Chinese
JUMPROPE

Anne Akers Johnson

KLUTZ®

KLUTZ

KLUTZ® creates activity books and other great stuff for kids ages 3 to 103. We began our corporate life in 1977 in a garage we shared with a Chevrolet Impala. Although we've outgrown that first office, Klutz galactic headquarters remains in Palo Alto, California, and we're still staffed entirely by real human beings. For those of you who collect mission statements, here's ours:

• Create wonderful things • Be good • Have fun

Write Us

We would love to hear your comments regarding this or any of our books. We have many!

KLUTZ.

450 Lambert Avenue
Palo Alto, CA 94306

Book printed in China. 112
Rope made in Taiwan.

ISBN 978-1-57054-098-1

9 3 7 0 4 2 4 5 1 4

Visit Our Website

You can check out all the stuff we make, find a nearby retailer, request a catalog, sign up for a newsletter, e-mail us or just goof off!
www.klutz.com

Distributed in the UK by
Scholastic UK Ltd
Westfield Road, Southam
Warwickshire, England CV47 0RA

Distributed in Australia by
Scholastic Australia Ltd
PO Box 579, Gosford
NSW Australia 2250

Distributed in Canada by
Scholastic Canada Ltd
604 King Street West, Toronto, Ontario
Canada M5V 1E1

Contents

The Basics

You need at least three people to play Chinese Jump Rope: two **enders** to hold the rope, and one **jumper**. There's no limit to how many players you can have in a game—just take turns so everyone gets a chance to jump.

Before you get started, find a nice clear area to play in. Move any rocks or gravel that might make you slip. Sidewalks are good. Make sure you have plenty of room to jump.

You'll do best if you play in comfy shoes that are easy to jump in and don't have slippery soles. Buckles or sandals can get caught on the ropes easily, making you miss. Good jumpers like to play in sneakers or other shoes that won't snag the ropes.

We've included two Chinese jump ropes with this book: a long one and a short one. Some games can only be played with the long one—we'll tell you when that's important. Otherwise, you can play with whichever rope you like. The short one is handy when you don't have a lot of room to spread out.

Most games start in the **Basic Position**.

The enders stand facing each other, with the rope running behind their ankles and their feet about a shoulder's width apart.

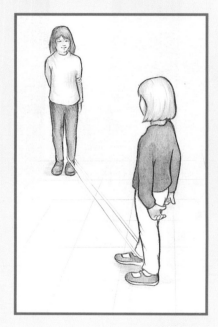

Another common starting position is **Skinnies**.

The enders face each other with the rope around just one leg.

Whatever the position, the rope should always be stretched just enough so that it doesn't droop. It will be too hard for the jumper if you stretch the rope too tightly.

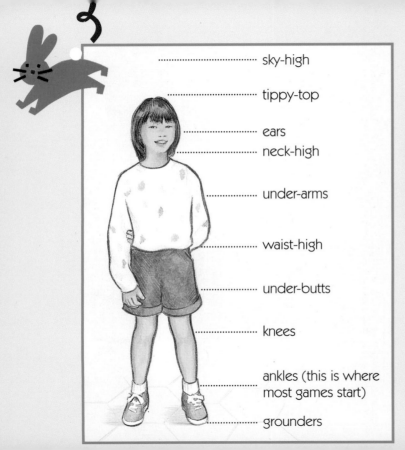

.... sky-high

.... tippy-top

.... ears
.... neck-high

.... under-arms

.... waist-high

.... under-butts

.... knees

.... ankles (this is where most games start)

.... grounders

There are ten different rope levels. Start with the easiest — usually ankles — and raise the rope to the next level after you finish a level without missing. Once you get past under-arms, it's best just to hold the rope at the right level in your hands.

Always be careful when you let go of the rope so that it doesn't snap back and hit the other ender.

The Rules

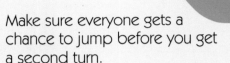

The rules are pretty much the same no matter which game you're playing.

We'll make you the first jumper. Play until you miss (a miss might mean stepping on a rope you weren't supposed to, landing in the wrong place, or getting your legs tangled while you're trying to jump out). The enders will be sure to let you know if you miss.

If you finish a level without missing, the enders should raise the rope to the next level and you can keep playing.

If you miss, your turn is over and you trade places with one of the enders.

Make sure everyone gets a chance to jump before you get a second turn.

When it's your turn to jump again, start at the level that you missed on before. If you made it all the way to knees before you missed, you start at knees on your next turn.

You won't often have a winner in Chinese Jump Rope, because it's almost impossible to jump all the levels. The important thing is to work at getting better and going on to the next level.

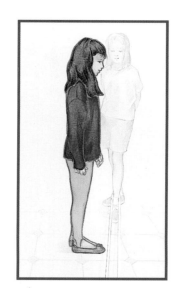

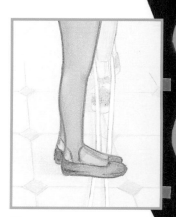

One Rope is always played with the rope around just one leg of each ender (skinnies). Start with the rope at ankle level, then keep moving it up to see how high you can go without missing.

1 Face the rope…

2 …then jump up and land on the near rope with both feet.

3 Now jump onto both ropes with both feet.

4 Scoot one foot forward and one back so that you have just one foot on each rope. Look at the picture to be sure you've got it right.

5 Pick up your forward foot and place it back on the near rope. You will be standing on this rope with both feet.

6 Turn your toes out so that the ropes slip out from under your feet.

7 End with a **Bunny Hop**. To do this, stand with your feet just under the near rope…

…jump up, picking up the near rope on your toes as you do…

…and land on the other side of the far rope (look at the picture).

To finish, jump up, let the rope slip off your feet, and land in the same spot.

*You can play almost any game with a partner—
this is called Doubles.*

Choose a game, then stand with your partner a few steps behind you, both facing the same way. Play the game together, making sure you both do all the steps at the same time.

Be careful not to kick each other! If either you or your partner misses, or if you don't do a jump at the same time, your team is out and the next team gets a chance to play.

Start this game at ankles, then keep raising the rope as high as you can. This game should be played fast, so once you get started, don't stop until you finish a level.

1
Start out in the basic position, with the rope to your right.

2 Tap into the center with your right foot.

3 Return this foot to its starting place.

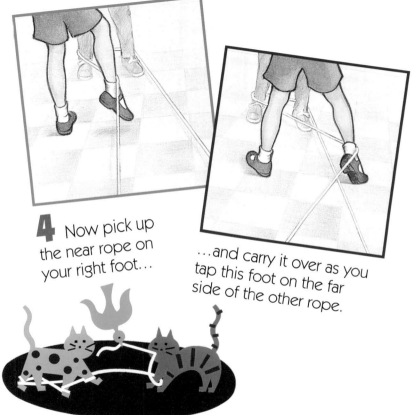

4 Now pick up the near rope on your right foot...

...and carry it over as you tap this foot on the far side of the other rope.

5 Return your right foot to its starting spot.

6 Repeat steps **2–5** two more times.

7 Do a **Sideways Jump**…

8 …so you land with your feet on either side of the far rope.

9 Lift your left foot out and place it beside your right foot.

10 Tap your left foot into the center of the ropes…

…then return it to its place beside your right foot.

11 Pick up the near rope with your left foot and tap on the other side of the far string…

12 …then step back out so your feet are together.

13 Repeat steps **10–12** twice.

14 Jump into the center with your feet together.

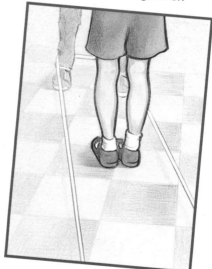

15 Then jump up and land with each foot on one string (look at the picture).

16 Jump up and land so your feet straddle the rope.

17 Now do a **Twisty Jump**.

To do this, squeeze your feet together...

...and turn around so you face the other ender.

Jump out, letting the strings slip off your ankles.

Be sure you land with your feet straddling the ropes.

18 Jump back over to the side you started on.

If you got this far without missing, move the ropes up to the knees of your enders and play the whole game all over again.

Teams

Any game can be played with teams as long as you have at least four players. Start by dividing into teams and deciding which team will start. The team that's not jumping makes two of its players enders.

The starting team lines up on one side of the rope. The first jumper plays the first level of the game. If she finishes without missing, she goes to the end of the line and lets her teammates take a turn at this level before she plays again. Everyone on the team must finish each level without missing or be "saved" by one of her teammates before the team can go on to the next level. Look at the next page to learn about "Saves."

Saves

When someone on your team misses, your team has one chance to save her. It doesn't matter which player is the saver.

To save someone, call out "Saves," then jump the level your teammate missed on. You can save just one person, or your whole team if you have to. Just be sure you call "Saves" first and be sure you jump the level once for every player you're saving. If you miss while you're trying to save someone, your team's turn is over. If you try to save, but don't call it first, it doesn't count and you have to do it over again.

Don't forget, after you've saved someone, you still have to jump the level for yourself. So if you save one player, you jump the level twice: once to save and once for yourself. If you miss on your turn, someone else can save you.

You'll need the long rope for this game. Unlike most games, this one starts at knee level, then goes down to ankles for the second, harder round. This is a good game to play in teams, though you can always play individually if you want. When playing teams, all of your teammates must complete each step before your team goes on to the next one.

1
Enders —
lay the rope
on the ground
in the shape
of an "8" and
step into it as
shown.

Then pull
the rope up
to your knees
and stand
with your
feet together
so it looks
like this:

Jumpers — The first step is a **Back-Kick** through the three ropes. To do this, hop from one foot to the other by kicking your feet back. Don't lift your knees to do this; just bend them as you kick back. Practice a couple of times without the rope first.

3 Hop over the middle ropes onto your right foot...

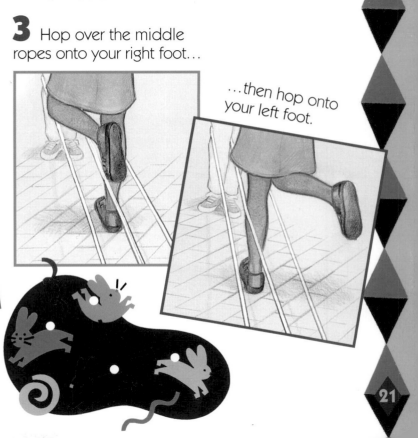

...then hop onto your left foot.

You have to do this step fast, and can't stop until you've finished it.

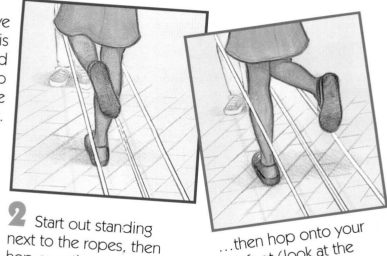

2 Start out standing next to the ropes, then hop over the first rope onto your right foot...

...then hop onto your left foot (look at the picture).

4 Hop over the far rope onto your right foot...

...then follow with your left foot.

You can rest now. If you're playing teams, go back to the starting side and wait until your teammates have all finished this step before going on.

The next step is **Overs**. It's okay to touch a rope while you're doing Overs, but if you land on a rope, or land in the wrong position, it's a miss.

5 Go back to your starting side and step your right foot over the near rope. Look at the picture to be sure you're starting in the right place.

6 Jump up and land so your feet straddle the middle ropes (check out the picture).

7 Now jump up and land so your feet straddle the far rope.

8 Jump out to the far side with both feet.

When everyone on your team has done Overs, go to the next step.

Next comes **Ons**:

9 Jump up and land on the first rope.

10 Jump off of this rope and land on the two middle ropes. This can get a little tricky!

If your feet are too big for this, try landing at an angle.

11 Now jump off the middle rope and land on the far rope with both feet.

Jump off this rope, then go back around to the starting side.

Next comes **Underjumps.**

12

Jump up, hooking the near rope on your feet...

...and land with both feet on the two middle ropes.

13 Keep that first rope hooked on your feet, and jump onto the far rope. If you land on any other rope, it's a miss!

14 Now jump all the way out to the far side, letting the ropes slip off your feet as you do. If the ropes don't slip off, or if you don't land in the right place, it's a miss.

When you've finished this level without missing, have the enders move the ropes down to their ankles and start over again from step **2**. This will be harder because the ropes will be even closer together.

You'll need the long rope and at least two teams of three to play this game. Decide which team will go first and which will hold the rope. Play the whole game at ankles, then go to knees, then under-butts if you're really good! Your whole team must finish each level without missing before you can go on to the next one. This is a good game to use Saves on (see page 19).

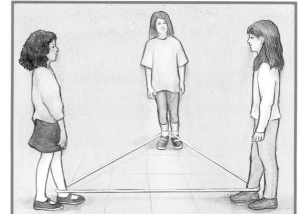

1 The team holding the rope stands in a triangle with the rope around one ankle.

Only one person can be on any one leg of the triangle at a time. If you and a teammate are ever playing on the same rope, it's a miss.

3 Now walk towards the next ender, being very careful not to touch the rope at all. If you touch it, it's a miss.

When you reach the next corner, stop and make sure your teammates are also at their corners. You all have to do the next step at the same time!

2 Jumpers, stand over the rope, each at a different corner of the triangle. Stand right next to the ender at your corner, with your back to her. Look at the picture to be sure you've got it right.

4 Lift your outside foot up and step over the next rope. Be careful not to touch it!

5 Walk around the triangle like this, until you get to the end of your last rope.

6 Now jump all the way over the next rope with both feet...

...so you land outside the triangle. You all have to do this together, so count to three, then jump.

7 Turn and face your rope, and on the count of three, jump onto it with both feet.

8 Walk along on top of the rope to the next corner. It will be easiest if you slide your feet along the rope.

9 When you get to the corner, jump onto the next rope with both feet. Make sure you all jump at the same time. If you don't land on the rope, it's a miss.

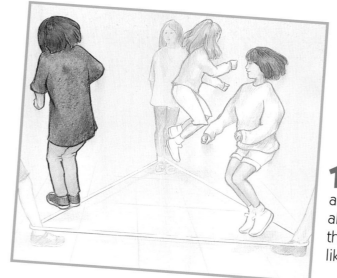

10 Walk and jump all around the triangle like this.

11 When you've reached the end of your last rope, count to three, then jump over the next rope...

...so you land outside the triangle.

12 If your team has come this far without making a mistake, move the rope up to the knees of your enders and repeat steps **2–11**. Jumping will be harder!

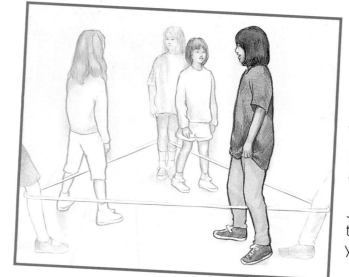

13 After knees, try under-butts. It's best if the enders just hold the rope in their hands at this level and stand back a bit, out of the way of the jumpers.

Jumpers, it's okay to touch the rope as you walk around on this level, but be careful you don't kick the enders when you're doing your jumps!

This is a team game. You can have as many players on a team as you want. Each player has to complete the jump before the team moves on to the next jump. If a jumper misses, a teammate can save her. But, as always, if the saving jumper misses, the team's turn is over. If you don't remember how Saves work, read page 19.

When your team's next turn comes up, you all have to start with the step that stumped your team before.

1

Start with the rope held on the ground by the enders as shown.

2 All of the jumpers take turns doing the first jump. Once you know how this jump goes, do it fast.

Jump up and land with your feet straddling the rope...

...then jump up and land with your feet crossed over the rope.

Repeat these steps once more: jump and straddle, jump and cross.

3 Finally, jump over to the far side so that your teammates can do the same jump.

4 When everyone on your team has either completed this first jump without missing, or been saved by someone else on the team, raise the rope up to the knees of the enders. It works best if the enders just hold the rope at their knees.

5

The next jump is a **Hoppy Jump**.

Jump over the rope and land on one foot.

Without putting your foot down, turn around and jump over the rope again, then turn around and jump once more. If you put your foot down before finishing the third jump, or if you don't make it over the rope, it's a miss.

6 When everyone on your team has had a chance to do this, move the rope up to under-butts.

7 Next, with the rope at under-butts, do three **Turning Jumps**. A Turning Jump goes like this:

Stand over the rope as shown.

Now jump up high and, while you're in the air, turn…

…so you land standing over the rope, but facing the other ender.

Do this two more times, then step off the rope so your teammates can give it a try.

8 Raise the rope up to the waists of the enders.

9

Back-Kick over the rope three times. To do this, stand right next to the rope. Kick the foot nearest the rope back and hook it over the rope. (Don't lift your knee, just bend it back!)

Hop onto this foot as you kick your other foot back and over the rope. It's okay to touch the rope at this level as long as you make it over.

10 If your team gets this far, you're really doing great! Move the rope up to the shoulders of the enders for the last and hardest step.

11 Now you're going to do three **Swingy Jumps** with the rope at under-arms. Use your hands to pull the rope down and hook it under one foot. This foot can't touch the ground until you've finished.

Without putting your rope foot down, jump backwards over the rope...

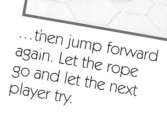

Swing this foot back as you jump over the rope with your other foot.

...then jump forward again. Let the rope go and let the next player try.

Make Your Own Rope

It's very easy to make your own Chinese jump rope using rubber bands. Your rope shouldn't be shorter than 28 inches, but there's no limit to how long it can be.

You will need about 40 rubber bands to make a small rope. The thicker they are, the stronger your rope will be.

If there's no one around to help you, find a sturdy chair leg to hold your rope as you work. If you have a human helper, make sure they don't let go of the end until you're finished.

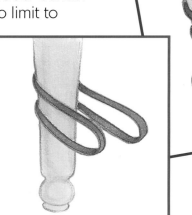

Start by folding a rubber band **1** around the leg of a chair as shown (or ask a friend to hold the first rubber band for you).

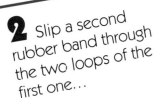

2 Slip a second rubber band through the two loops of the first one…

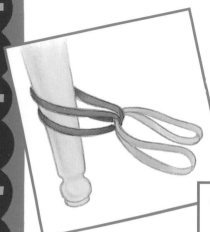

3 ...then fold this rubber band in half.

4 Continue adding rubber bands like this until the rope is as long as you want it. Slip the first rubber band off the chair leg, being careful not to let the rope unravel.

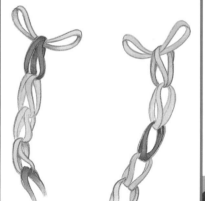

5 Slip one more rubber band through all four loops of the end rubber bands.

6

Knot this rubber band a couple of times to hold it together.

You can make the rope as long as you want, and can use it for any game in this book. If it breaks after a while, just tie it together with another rubber band.

This game is played by hopping from foot to foot. You have to hop fast and, once you start, you should never be standing on more than one foot at a time.

1 Start with the enders in the basic position.

2 Hop into the center on your right foot...

3 ...then hop back out on your left foot.

4 Hop across both ropes with your right foot...

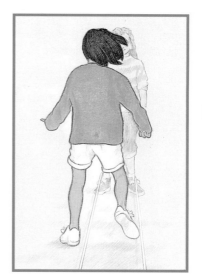

5 ...then hop back out onto your left foot.

6 Hop back into the center with your right foot...

7

...then hop back out on your left foot.

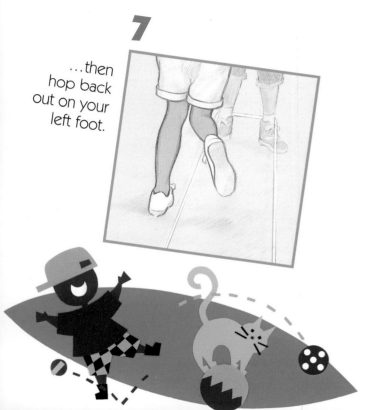

8 Now, without stopping, pick up the near rope on your right foot and carry it over as you hop to the far side.

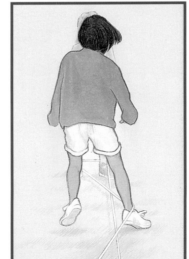

9 Hop back onto your left foot.

10 Hop into the center on your right foot…

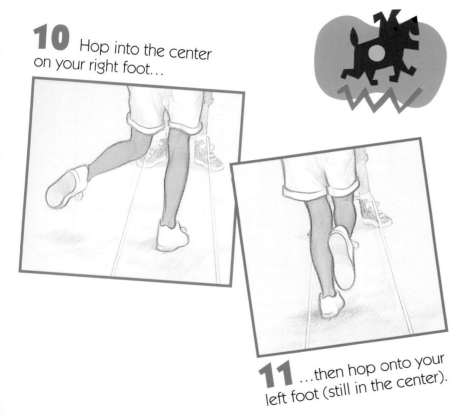

11 …then hop onto your left foot (still in the center).

12 Hop to the far side on your right foot…

13 …then follow with your left foot.

Now you're on the other side of the ropes. Do the same thing on this side, only this time you will start off with your left foot.

Andrea's favorite

Start this game at ankles, then go to knees.
This is a great game to play with a partner (see page 11).

1 Start with the enders in the basic position.

Stand with your right foot in the center and your left foot outside the ropes as shown.

2 Jump crosswise (so your feet land on either side of the far rope).

3 Now jump back to your starting position.

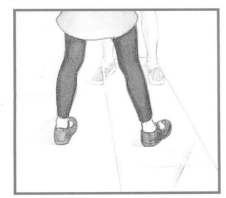

4 Do two more crosswise jumps like this so you end up in your starting position.

5 Jump into the middle with both feet.

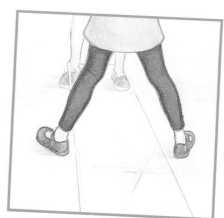

6 Jump out so your feet straddle the ropes.

7

Then jump up and land with one foot on top of each string as shown.

8 Jump out so your feet straddle the ropes.

9 Do a **Twisty Jump**:

Then jump up and out of the ropes...

...landing so your feet straddle both ropes.

To do this, scoot your feet together and turn around to face the other ender. The rope will wrap around your ankles.

10 Do another Twisty Jump. Remember to land with your feet straddling the ropes.

11 Now do a
Diamond Jump:

Pick up the near rope with your right foot and lift it up and over the other rope.

Step your left foot into the center of the two ropes, then spread your feet to make a diamond out of the rope.

Jump out and let the ropes slip off your feet. Land so your feet straddle the ropes. If the rope is still around either ankle, you missed!

12 Do another Diamond Jump.

13 Jump over to one side and get ready for a **Bunny Jump**.

Start by standing with your toes just under the near rope…

…then jump up, pick up the near rope on your toes…

…and land on the other side of the far rope. You should have a rope on your ankles.

Finally, end the Bunny Jump by jumping up and letting the rope drop off your ankles.

14 Turn around and do one more Bunny Jump.

If you get this far without making a mistake, move the rope up to the knees of your enders and do it some more.

After knees, turn the page and go on to Toothpicks.

After you've finished Andrea's Favorite at knee level, try Toothpicks. The game is almost the same, but the enders hold the rope in skinnies.

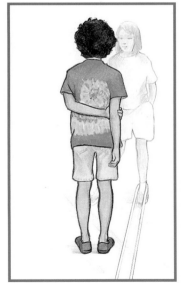

1 Have the enders put the rope around one ankle each, so the two ropes are really close together.

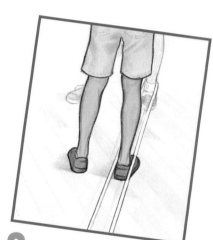

2 Step into the center with your right foot, as shown in the picture.

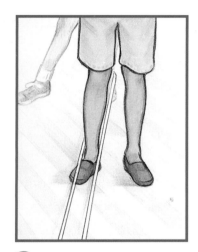

3 Lift your left foot and step all the way over to the other side of the rope, turning as you go so you face the other ender.

4 Do this three more times fast. (Don't get dizzy!) You should end up facing the ender you started out facing.

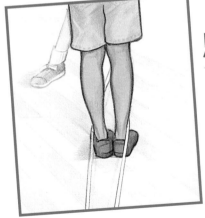

5 Step into the center with your left foot, so that both feet are inside the ropes.

6 Jump out with both feet and land so you straddle the ropes.

7 Jump up and land on both ropes with both feet.

8 Now jump up and land with your feet straddling the ropes.

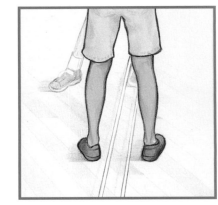

9 Do a **Twisty Jump** by scooting your feet together, turning to face the other ender…

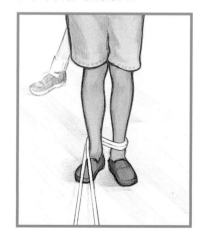

10

…then jumping up and letting the ropes slip off your ankles. Land straddling the ropes.

Do another Twisty Jump. You'll end up facing the ender you were facing when you started.

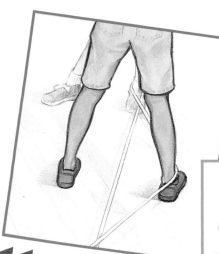

11 Now do a **Diamond Jump**: Pick up the near rope with your right foot and lift it up and over the other rope...

...then step your left foot into the center of the two ropes. Spread your feet to make a diamond out of the rope...

...then jump out of the diamond and land so your feet straddle the ropes.

12 Do another Diamond Jump.

13 Do a **Bunny Jump**.
(This is harder when you're doing Toothpicks!)

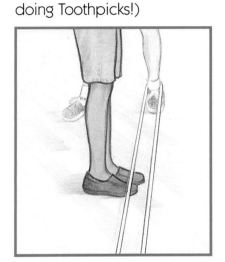

Start by standing with your toes just under the near rope…

…then jump over the far rope, hooking the near rope, on your ankle as you go.

Jump up in place and let the rope slip off your ankle.

14 Turn around so you face the rope, then do one more Bunny Jump.

When you've played this game without missing at ankle level, go on to knees (still Toothpicks!).

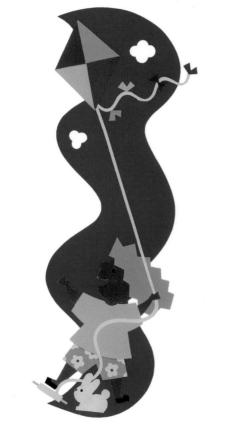

Limbo is a team game, so start out by dividing into two teams, then decide which team gets to go first. Two people who aren't on the starting team act as enders, but instead of putting the rope around their legs as they usually would, they hold the rope in one hand at each level. Start with grounders and go all the way to sky high if you can.

The starting team lines up on one side of the rope, and takes turns jumping over the rope at each level. When it's your turn, jump over the rope, then run back around to the end of the line on the starting side.

Your team can't raise the rope to the next level until each team player has successfully jumped over the rope. It's okay to do Saves (see page 19 if you aren't sure how), but remember, if four people on your team miss a level, the saver has to jump over four times without missing, then once more for herself. If the saver misses, your team is out and the other team gets a chance to jump.

1 It doesn't matter how you jump over, but at grounders, ankles and knees you can't touch the rope or it's a miss.

You can hop over...

...or leap over.

2 When the rope gets up to under-butts, it's okay to touch the rope with your feet and legs (no hands!) as long as you don't step on it.
A good way to get over is to use the **Back-Kick**.

To do this, kick your leg back at the knee and hook your foot over the rope...

...then hop over, as you kick your left leg back and over the rope. Remember, you don't lift your legs, you just kick your foot back.

3 As the rope gets higher, especially after waist-high, the only way to get over the rope is by turning a cartwheel over it. Remember, on these higher levels, it's okay to touch the rope as long as you don't land on it.

If not everyone on your team can do a cartwheel, someone else will have to do cartwheel Saves for them.

Thanks to the Chinese jump ropers at Cabrillo and Jefferson Elementary Schools in San Francisco, Sakamoto Elementary in San Jose, and to all the jumpers right here at Klutz Galactic Headquarters. Thanks also to Sandy Cohen-Winn, Andrea Judge, and Corie Thompson.

Cover Art and
Interior Illustrations:
Mary Thelen

Instructional Drawings:
Sara Boore

Art Direction:
MaryEllen Podgorski

Design:
Nelson Design

Ridiculous
Suggestions:
John Cassidy

Can't get enough?

Here are some simple ways to keep the Klutz coming.

1. **Order more Chinese Jump Ropes** at klutz.com. It's quick, it's easy and, seriously, where else are you going to find jump ropes just like the ones on this book?

2. Get your hands on a copy of **The Klutz Catalog**. To request a free copy of our mail order catalog, go to klutz.com/catalog.

3. Become a **Klutz Insider** and get e-mail about new releases, special offers, contests, games, goofiness and who-knows-what-all. If you're a grown-up who wants to receive e-mail from Klutz, head to klutz.com/insider.

If any of this sounds good to you, but you don't feel like going online right now, just give us a call at 1-800-737-4123. We'd love to hear from you.

More Great Books from Klutz

My Style Studio: Design & Trace Your Own Fashions

Just Between Us • Paper-craft Cards • Paper Fashions

It's All About Me: Personality Quizzes for You and Your Friends

Capsters™ • Cat's Cradle® A Book of String Figures

The Incredble Clay Book® • The Cootie Catcher Book

Friendship Bracelets • Face Painting

Made You Look • My Very Own Horse Book

Me and My Friends: The Book of Us

My Life According to Me® • Nail Art

Origami • Potholders and Other Loopy Projects

Scoubidou • Shrink Art Jewelry

The Spiral Draw Book • Spool Knit Jewelry

Stencil Art • Window Art